ALSO AVAILABLE IN THIS SERIES:
DREAM: The Words and Inspiration of Martin Luther King, Jr.
LOVE: The Words and Inspiration of Mother Teresa
BELIEVE: The Words and Inspiration of Desmond Tutu

Produced and originated by PQ Blackwell Limited
116 Symonds Street, Auckland, New Zealand
www.pqblackwell.com

Distributed exclusively in the United States, Canada, and the Philippines by Blue
Mountain Arts, Inc.

Concept, design, and essay copyright © 2007 PQ Blackwell Limited.
Introduction copyright © 2007 Desmond M. Tutu.

Designed by Cameron Gibb, Annatjie Matthee, and Carolyn Lewis.

Printed by Midas Printing International Ltd., China.

Library of Congress Control Number: 2006909706
ISBN: 978-1-59842-242-9

Certain trademarks are used under license.
BLUE MOUNTAIN PRESS is registered in U.S. Patent and Trademark Office.

Acknowledgments appear on page 94.

First Printing: 2007

Blue Mountain Arts, Inc.
P.O. Box 4549, Boulder, Colorado 80306

THE WORDS AND INSPIRATION OF

MAHATMA GANDHI

INTRODUCTION BY
ARCHBISHOP DESMOND TUTU

Blue Mountain Press ®

Boulder, Colorado

"If I diminish you, I diminish myself."

In my culture and tradition the highest praise that can be given to someone is, "*Yu, u nobuntu,*" an acknowledgment that he or she has this wonderful quality: *ubuntu*. It is a reference to their actions toward their fellow human beings, it has to do with how they regard people and how they see themselves within their intimate relationships, their familial relationships, and within the broader community. *Ubuntu* addresses a central tenet of African philosophy: the essence of what it is to be human.

The definition of this concept has two parts. The first is that the person is friendly, hospitable, generous, gentle, caring, and compassionate. In other words, someone who will use their strengths on behalf of others — the weak and the poor and the ill — and not take advantage of anyone. This person treats others as he or she would be treated. And because of this they express the second part of the concept, which concerns openness, large-heartedness. They share their worth. In doing so my humanity is recognized and becomes inextricably bound to theirs.

People with *ubuntu* are approachable and welcoming; their attitude is kindly and well-disposed; they are not threatened by the goodness in others because their own esteem and self-worth is generated by knowing they belong to a greater whole. To recast the Cartesian proposition "I think, therefore I am," *ubuntu* would phrase it, "I am human because I belong." Put another way, "a person is a person through other people," a concept perfectly captured by the phrase "me we." No one comes into the world fully formed. We would not know how to think or walk or speak or behave unless we learned it from our fellow human beings. We need other human beings in order to be human. The solitary, isolated human being is a contradiction in terms.

Because we need one another, our natural tendency is to be cooperative and helpful. If this were not true we would have died out as a species long ago, consumed by our violence and hate. But we haven't. We have kept on despite the evil and the wars that have brought so much suffering and misery down the centuries. We have kept on because we strive for harmony and community, a community not only of the living but also one that honors our forebears. This link to the past gives us a sense of continuity, a sense that we have created, and create societies that are meant to be for the greater good and try to overcome anything that subverts our purpose. Our wars end; we seek to heal.

But anger, resentment, a lust for revenge, greed, even the aggressive competitiveness that rules so much of our contemporary world, corrodes and jeopardizes our harmony. *Ubuntu* points out that those who seek to destroy and dehumanize are also victims — victims, usually, of a pervading ethos, be it a political ideology, an economic system, or a distorted religious conviction. Consequently, they are as much dehumanized as those on whom they trample.

Never was this more obvious than during the apartheid years in South Africa. All humanity is interlinked. Thus, the humanity of the perpetrators of apartheid was inexorably bound to that of their victims. When they dehumanized another by inflicting suffering and harm, they dehumanized themselves. In fact I said at the time that the oppressor was dehumanized as much as, if not more than, those oppressed. How else could you interpret the words of the minister of police, Jimmy Kruger, on hearing of the death of Black Consciousness leader, Steve Biko, in prison. Of his tortured and painful killing, Kruger said, it "leaves me cold." You have to ask what has happened to the humanity — the *ubuntu* — of someone who could speak so callously about the suffering and death of a fellow human being.

It was equally clear that recovering from this situation would require a magnanimousness on the part of the victims if there was to be a future. The end of apartheid, I knew, would put *ubuntu* to the test. Yet I never doubted its power of reconciliation. In fact I often recalled the words of a man called Malusi Mpumlwana, an associate of Biko's, who, even while he was being tortured by the security police, looked at his torturers and realized that these were human beings too and that they needed him "to help them recover the humanity they [were] losing."

This is the essence of *ubuntu*, or "me we," and it is expressed so poignantly in the life and actions of the Mahatma Gandhi. In a long lifetime he made personal sacrifices that constantly revealed his compassion and concern for others. Everything he did was a demonstration of *ubuntu* — he was driven to help the poor, the sick, and the downtrodden and to free them from colonialism no matter the cost to himself. In the end it cost him his life. However, he left us a legacy of inspiration that is remarkable in its sincerity and love of humanity.

His *ubuntu* showed that the only way we can ever be human is together. The only way we can be free is together.

The Most Reverend Desmond M. Tutu, OMSG DD FKC
Anglican Archbishop Emeritus of Cape Town

Mahatma Gandhi

Mohandas Karamchand Gandhi

1869 – 1948

At the age of sixty-one, Mohandas Gandhi, wearing a homespun dhoti, walked two hundred and forty miles to the sea at Dandi to scoop up a small handful of natural salt. For twenty-six days this small, scrawny man with a staff in his hand trudged through the heat and dust from village to village. At each settlement he would encourage people to wear dhotis made of a hand-woven cloth called *khadi*, to treat the Untouchables as equals, to foreswear drink and drugs, to improve sanitation, and to break the salt monopoly imposed by Britain.

Each evening he would work at his spinning wheel, prepare speeches, and give interviews before retiring at nine to sleep. In the morning, again he would set out at the head of a procession that had been seventy-eight chosen followers in the beginning, but had soon grown to thousands. Among them were women, both poor and wealthy, although Gandhi had originally not wanted women on the march, fearing a violent reprisal from the British forces. As it happened the violence never materialized, but the Salt March became an event publicized around the world. Gandhi's purpose — to have the hated "Salt Law" repealed and with it an onerous tax — gathered support with each step he took.

"The tax shows itself still more burdensome on the poor man when it is remembered that salt is the one thing he must eat more than the rich man," he wrote to the viceroy, Lord Irwin, in early March 1930, ten days before his pilgrimage began. Adding, "My ambition is no less than to convert the British people through nonviolence, and thus make them see the wrong they have done to India. I do not seek to harm your people. I want to serve them even as I want to serve my own people... If the [Indian] people join me as I expect they will, the sufferings they will undergo, unless the British nation soon retraces its steps, will be enough to melt the stoniest hearts."[1]

Words in Gandhi's hands were always good tools, but for him they were never enough. Without action they were meaningless, as the Salt March proved. In the aftermath, the impact of his action rolled across the country and people began collecting natural salt, demonstrating outside liquor stores, burning foreign cloth. Inevitably their actions met with police retaliation: demonstrators were beaten, imprisoned, shot. Gandhi wrote in protest at the brutality and police violence until he, too, was arrested. But something had changed in the hearts of ordinary Indians: civil disobedience against the "Salt Law" had given them the strength to defy their colonial overlords. And although independence was still seventeen years away, a new spirit was unleashed.

In a lifetime of heroic stands against injustice and exploitation it is difficult to single out a moment that had more value than others, but perhaps the symbolic power and emotional immediacy of the Salt March offer an exceptional insight into Gandhi. Gandhi himself felt he was on the cusp of something important, telling a vast audience on the night before he set out from his ashram: "This will be my last speech on the sacred banks of the Sabarmati [River]. Possibly these may be the last words of my life here."[2] As it turned out they weren't, but that does not lessen the depth of his feeling.

The entire twenty-four day journey represents Gandhi at his most expressive. He wore a dhoti — the simple loincloth — made of *khadi*. And each day he spun cloth on his own loom. Both his dress and this activity were indicative of Gandhi's love for his fellow citizens and his desire to find practical ways to help an increasingly impoverished nation. The reasons behind adopting the *khadi* were threefold: an attempt to stimulate a weaving industry that had fallen away because of the prevalence of manufactured cloth, to create a demand for Indian yarn, and, in an overt way, to identify with the peasants and poor. No doubt too, his advocacy of hand spinning was a demonstration of his resistance to industrialization.

When Gandhi first became interested in *khadi* in 1915, spinning wheels had long been abandoned, and the skill had all but disappeared. It remained, however, in the hands of a few women scattered about the vast rural areas. So he sought out these women and learned the craft and then proceeded to propagate it wherever he went. "I swear by this," he told a cotton mill owner who had come to protest that Gandhi's "*khadi* movement" would adversely affect production at the mills, "because through it I can provide work to the semi-starved, semi-employed women of India."[3] In a country where millions spent most of the year unoccupied, spinning cloth seemed to Gandhi a way of bolstering their meager incomes. He had already dispensed with his British-made suits and turban in favor of the dhoti, but now began wearing loincloths made from the coarse homespun *khadi*.

For Gandhi, spinning also had a spiritual significance. In fact it became a daily activity that bordered on an obsession. For him it was a time of meditation and of self-improvement, a time when he could identify with those who were poor or earned their livelihoods through manual labor. It was also his way of expressing his concern for the Untouchables of a caste system that he detested. For an hour each day he sat at his loom to demonstrate his solidarity. But more than this, he wanted all Indians to spin for at least half an hour a day as a way of expressing their commitment, as a way of conferring dignity on manual labor and as a way of confirming their desire for self-rule. He wanted the spinning wheel to become a symbol of national unity.

And even on that long, hot march to the salt pans at Dandi, Gandhi did not neglect his central focus: if he was to help his fellow citizens, then he had to be at one with them.

By the time of the Salt March in March 1930, Gandhi had long been a national figure of hope and inspiration in India and a man with an international reputation. He had been leader of the major political party, the Indian National Congress, and in many ways he was still a unifying force within a party that was anything but consolidated in its politics. But it was his ideals, or more particularly, his expression of those ideals that gave Gandhi his stature. It was, too, the consistency of his actions. The foundations for this attitude toward his fellow humans had been forged during the twenty-one years he spent in South Africa from 1893 to 1914.

Despite the abiding photographic images of Gandhi in a dhoti, he had been born in 1869 into a middle-class Hindu family and a comfortable three-story house that was shared with an extended family. He was the youngest child of his father's fourth wife, and as a schoolboy he was extremely shy not only with adults but also with his contemporaries. According to Hindu custom, at the age of thirteen he was married, although he and his wife were to spend little time together during their first five years. His bride, Kasturbai Makanji, a headstrong girl, was slightly younger than Gandhi, and he soon became jealous of her independent spirit. In their first year of marriage his schoolwork deteriorated and he failed to take the year-end examination. On promising to apply himself, he was readmitted at a higher grade, although he was never more than an average student.

While the young Gandhi was both absorbed and intrigued by his marriage — a marriage that was to last sixty-two years — the older Gandhi came to see child marriage as a "cruel custom"[4] that subjected children to the unnecessary distractions of lust and jealousy. "I can see no moral argument in support of such a preposterously early marriage," he wrote in his autobiography.[5]

However, the teenage Gandhi, battling with his jealousy and his lust, was also as much given to impetuous behavior as any teenager. For instance, his parents were vegetarians, but he would occasionally indulge in "meat feasts" with his friends — although these feasts often disturbed his sleep with nightmares of bleating goats. These aftereffects were among the reasons he committed himself to vegetarianism at the age of nineteen. Another escapade, although one with more serious moral consequences for the fifteen-year-old Gandhi, led him to steal some gold from his father to pay off a debt incurred by his brother. The theft so perturbed Gandhi that he confessed to his father in writing, acknowledging his guilt, asking for punishment, and pledging never to steal again. His father, deeply moved by this confession, tore up the note and wept. Later, Gandhi was to see this reaction as an object lesson in *ahimsa* — nonviolence toward all living things.

Once he had finished school, Gandhi left India to study law in London. His time there was lonely and difficult. Although he was attracted to the culture, he found English manners and mores baffling. Similarly, his strict adherence to vegetarianism in a society given to meat-eating meant that his meals were bland. Nevertheless, he applied himself to his studies and was called to the bar in June 1891. Two days later he returned to India, glad to be going home despite an affection for London that would last his lifetime.

Establishing a legal practice in India was not as easy as he had imagined. Despite his qualifications, he lacked a knowledge of Indian law and, more importantly, became intimidated to the point of speechlessness in public or even before a small group of people — not a characteristic that made for a good lawyer. At his first case he was too overawed to say anything.

With his prospects looking decidedly unattractive, Gandhi accepted an offer from a mercantile firm that required a legal representative with knowledge of the English language and English law in their office in the British colony of Natal. He was not overly perturbed at leaving his wife and their two children for a year, and was almost relieved to be away from India. In fact, he looked forward to being in a new country. This new country was the place where Gandhi would acquire a voice and first demonstrate his feelings for the marginalized and the downtrodden. He arrived in Natal at the port of Durban on May 23, 1893. His one year would become several years, with his wife and family later joining him.

Natal in the last decade of the nineteenth century was one of a collection of British colonies and Boer republics that would eventually make up modern South Africa. In this agglomeration of states, an uneasy truce existed between the indigenous population and the settlers, while at two makeshift towns, Kimberley (with its diamonds) and Johannesburg (with its gold), tensions between the two settler groups, the Boers and the British, were at the breaking point. Soon the Boer republics would go to war against Britain and, only three years later on the cessation of hostilities, a unified South Africa would be established. That unity brought with it a systematic racist policy that stripped the indigenous population of their land and designated everyone with a skin color other than white as second-class citizens. This was the cauldron into which Gandhi had unwittingly pitched himself.

Natal in 1893 had a small Indian population as a result of the importation of indentured Indian laborers a few decades earlier to work the sugar cane fields. Their numbers had increased marginally as immigrants continued to dribble into the colony. Conditions for Indians were, if not enticing, at least not obstructionist: they were regarded as ordinary citizens with rights to property, to conduct business, to travel freely, and some even qualified for the franchise. However, beneath the surface, the racial tension was fraught, as Gandhi soon discovered in a revelation that determined much of what was to follow.

He had not been in Natal long before he was required to travel to Pretoria on legal business. He booked a first-class train fare from Durban, but a white passenger boarding at Pietermaritzburg two hours later objected to travelling in a carriage with an Indian. Railway officials were summoned, and Gandhi was instructed to move to the third-class van at the end of the train reserved for dark-skinned people. He protested that he had a first-class ticket, but the officials were unmoved. In the end he was forcibly ejected by the police and dumped on the station. It was nine o'clock on a bitterly cold winter night. Humiliated, Gandhi spent a wretched night in the station waiting room. Throughout the shivering hours he agonized: should he fight for his rights or go back to India? To run back to India was cowardice, he decided. Better to stay. "The hardship to which I was subjected was superficial — only a symptom of the deep disease of color prejudice. I should try, if possible, to root out the disease and suffer hardships in the process. Redress for wrongs I should seek only to the extent that would be necessary for the removal of the color prejudice."[6] These words in his autobiography are virtually a summary of how he was to approach all the obstacles and challenges in his life.

The next day, after the intercession of his business friends, Gandhi was allowed to travel on to Pretoria in a first-class carriage. However, the last stretch of the journey was by horse-drawn coach, and Gandhi once again was met with hard racist attitudes. The coachman regarded him as a "coolie" and coolies could not travel in the box with white passengers. He was forced to sit on an outside seat for the duration of the coach ride.

The months Gandhi spent in Pretoria working on a legal case were not demanding, and he was able to devote much time to reading and meeting with fellow Indians. His shyness had evaporated, as if his experiences on the train and coach trip had given him not only confidence but a mission. Yet, significantly, the first "political" speech he made was not about human rights or the inequities of racial discrimination, but almost a plea to his audience of (mostly Muslim) merchants to be truthful, to learn English, and to be scrupulously clean in their habits and houses. Gandhi had seen how Indians were confined to ghettos and was appalled both by the lack of sanitation and by their irresponsible sanitary habits. Cleanliness was to be one of his major fixations for the rest of his life. He felt the merchants should learn English for they would otherwise never be able to express their grievances. At that meeting he also exhorted the merchants to be tolerant of Indians who were Hindus and Christians. Probably there was nothing in these sentiments that his audience hadn't heard before, but they had not heard them spoken with such conviction and passion. What they heard impressed them. When Gandhi suggested they form an association to represent their views and hardships, the merchants quickly accepted. For his part, he vowed to devote as much of his time as he could in their service. He was twenty-three. Importantly, he was beginning to see his role not only as that of the advocate but also of the campaigner. Asking people to adopt certain principles was insufficient; he would show them how.

The legal case Gandhi was pursuing on his employer's behalf also had an encouraging outcome. The judge found in their favor and instructed the defendant to pay the outstanding money and all legal costs. However, the defendant now faced bankruptcy. Perturbed by this, Gandhi convinced his employer to allow the repayments to be made in easy installments, and the compromise suited both parties. "I realized that the true function of a lawyer was to unite parties riven asunder," Gandhi recorded in his autobiography. "The lesson was so indelibly burnt into me that a large part of my time during the twenty years of my practice as a lawyer was occupied in bringing about private compromises of hundreds of cases." Here was the Gandhi of the future: the man who could see all sides of a problem and would seek compromises that offered a dignified solution to all parties. If the Gandhi who set out for Pretoria was the chrysalis, then the man who emerged at the end of his months in that city was the butterfly — a butterfly that would touch the lives of many.

To extend the butterfly metaphor, Gandhi was drawn to people — especially the marginalized — as the butterfly is drawn to flowers. He wanted to acknowledge their suffering and to bring promise into their lives. And there were three fundamental ways in which he did this: he identified with poor people in his personal circumstances and behavior; he sought out the neglected in their homes no matter how remote or degraded these might be; and he acted on their behalf even if that meant personal suffering, which invariably it did. His life can be seen as iconic: he stood for others. And the essence of these attitudes toward his fellows can be traced back to his early political life.

Gandhi had been in Natal for two years and had already become a major figure in local Indian politics by helping to found the Natal Indian Congress when he visited a Trappist settlement at Mariannhill outside Durban. The settlement comprised almost two hundred monks and nuns and over a thousand Zulus, including women and children. What impressed Gandhi was the absence of race or class distinctions and the lack of personal possessions. Everyone ate the same food, worked together in the fields, and slept in a large hall. He responded to the serenity of the surroundings and the community's self-supporting independence. There was a school, vegetable gardens, and bakeries. He was also inspired by the rigorous devotion and vegetarianism of the Trappist monks. Gandhi spent only a day there, but eight years later that day led to his purchasing — with the help of several rich Indians — a tract of land twenty kilometers outside Durban, called Phoenix.

Initially Gandhi offered sanctuary at Phoenix to those friends and relations who had come from India with him. There were also some Zulus living in huts on the property who he allowed to remain. While the ideal was to give people an opportunity to live a simple and natural life in the beautiful countryside, the reality was that Phoenix had to be financed from the proceeds of Gandhi's thriving legal practices in Johannesburg and Durban and by a newspaper, the *Indian Opinion*, he had founded. While he desired the life of a peasant, he was still trapped by the commercial world.

But Gandhi's thoughts, influenced by his daily readings in the *Bhagavad Gita* and of tracts by writers such as John Ruskin and Tolstoy, particularly Tolstoy's

Letter to a Hindu, were increasingly attracted by the concepts of *aparigraha* (nonpossession) and *samabhava* (equability). Ruskin held that the good of the individual was contained in the good of all, that all work was equal, and that the life of manual labor was a worthy life. These were concepts dear to Gandhi, who was already living and practicing the principles of *satyagraha* (the force of truth and love) and *ahimsa* (nonviolence), as his political activities brought him up against the racist forces of the fledgling South African state. Initially he thought of his opposition as passive resistance but changed this to the *satyagraha* struggle with the emphasis on nonviolence, truth, and love. As this struggle developed, Gandhi increasingly felt the need for another center that demonstrated his ideals. When he was given land near Johannesburg, he immediately started a settlement called Tolstoy Farm in honor of the Russian writer's polemic, *The Kingdom of God Is Within You*. This time there were no restrictions; it was open to whomever wished to live there provided they abided by its ethic.

Tolstoy Farm was closely aligned to the principles of self-sufficiency practiced at the Trappist retreat that had so impressed Gandhi. The community grew their own food, made their own clothing (including sandals which they also sold), were strict vegetarians, and organized a school for the children. Although Gandhi still ran his legal firm, he believed he was moving closer to his ideal of serving the people.

Phoenix and Tolstoy Farm were the forerunners to the Satyagraha Ashram Gandhi would found in India when he finally left South Africa in 1915. His return was mostly for family reasons — his brother had died, and in the patriarchal custom he was now head of the family — although the South African government was relieved to see the last of him.

Gandhi slipped immediately into Indian political life by launching his *satyagraha* movement. His first priority, however, was to found an ashram.

He toured the country, travelling third class, wearing his now trademark dhoti. He was welcomed in the various centers as a hero, such was the power of the reputation he had gained in South Africa. He eventually chose land outside the town of Ahmedabad for an ashram that was managed by one of the people who had helped him establish Phoenix. Its exacting constitution demanded, among other conditions, truth telling, celibacy, *ahimsa*, nonpossession, and acceptance of Untouchables.

Gandhi's attitudes toward Untouchables had manifested early in his life. As a prepubescent he had told his mother that untouchability was not sanctioned by religion. Already the Indian caste system had troubled him. Many years later in Natal, in the large house he ran before the founding of Phoenix, he was happy to give accommodation to Untouchables. This led to tensions with his wife, Kasturbai, who was less tolerant, especially over the issue of cleaning chamber pots. There were no toilets in the house so chamber pots were used in the upstairs rooms. A roster system meant that everyone in the house — Gandhi included — was scheduled to clear these pots, even that of the Untouchable, from time to time. Kasturbai couldn't bring herself to do this, which shocked Gandhi.

If Kasturbai was appalled in that instance, she was to be further incensed at the Satyagraha Ashram when an Untouchable couple with their baby daughter were admitted into the community. Some ashramites, despite their vows, could not abide the family's presence. They felt humiliated and degraded merely to be associated with them. To stop the tension, Gandhi adopted the young couple's daughter. But the matter didn't stop there. The textile merchants who had been financing the ashram withdrew their funds in protest of this defiled community. Gandhi responded that if necessary he would move the ashram into the Untouchable quarter of Ahmedabad and would live from the produce of their labor.

For Gandhi, Hinduism was denigrated by its insistence on the Untouchable caste system. Throughout his life he railed against this injustice, and in 1932, while imprisoned on a charge of civil disobedience, he took a political stand on behalf of the Untouchables by vowing to fast to death unless they were included among the Hindu section of the proposed Central Assembly. "My fight against untouchability is a fight against the impure in humanity," he told newspaper reporters in a rare interview at the time.[8] By then he was weak, spending his days in the shade of a mango tree in the prison yard. Yet his commitment brought political changes for the Untouchables: it opened to them temple doors and water wells across the nation and led to the observance of an Untouchability Abolition Week. Perhaps inevitably, many of these rights were later rescinded, but a crack had manifested in the edifice, even though Gandhi felt obliged to fast again and again on their behalf in the coming years.

This empathy for others was Gandhi's defining characteristic. From the moment on that cold Pietermaritzburg railway station when he decided to fight against inequality and discrimination, he opened his heart to his fellow human beings. This compassion showed itself in his urge to meet people during his Pretoria days and led those he came into contact with to unburden their suffering to him. And Gandhi listened to whomever needed to be heard. When he returned to India he traveled extensively, always by the humblest means, often walking if there was no transport, with the simple purpose of talking to those he met and finding out how they lived. Even in Britain in 1931, while on a political mission where he was scheduled to meet the powerful and the influential, he set aside time to walk the slum streets of London's East End and the depressed textile towns of Lancashire, where he listened attentively to the stories of the jobless and the poor.

Gathering and uplifting the oppressed was one of Gandhi's strengths and indicative of his benevolence. It was internationally apparent during the famous Salt March, but it had first expressed itself in what became known as the "Army of Peace." In October 1913, at the head of more than two thousand men, women, and children, Gandhi set out on a three hundred kilometer march from the Natal town of Newcastle to Tolstoy Farm. He and his "army" were protesting against a poll tax that had been imposed on Indian laborers. In the first four days of the march Gandhi was arrested three times and finally imprisoned for having induced civil unrest. Eventually the march was stopped, but indentured laborers across the country went on strike and the government was forced to rescind the tax. On his release from prison, Gandhi appeared before a gathering wearing a dhoti and sandals. He had forsaken Western clothing, he told the crowds, in sympathy with those who had been shot during the strike. The thin, short man in the dhoti instantly became the hero of the disenfranchised.

Similarly Gandhi's humanity revealed itself in his desire to heal people. Before turning to law he had contemplated studying medicine, and in his Phoenix days he read extensively on herbal and natural remedies. When a mysterious and deadly disease broke out among the Indian community in Johannesburg, Gandhi was quick to nurse the sick and the dying despite the risk of contagion. In this spirit of service, he joined the Red Cross during the Anglo-Boer War, and at the outbreak of the First World War he organized Indian volunteers to serve in the British Army's Field Ambulance Corps.

But perhaps Gandhi's greatest demonstration of his humanity was his willingness to suffer on behalf of others. Inevitably this meant coming into conflict with the authorities, and this in turn meant arrest and incarceration. The first occasion was in Johannesburg in 1907 in defiance of an act of parliament that greatly curtailed the freedom of Indians. He was sentenced to two months' hard labor. He was to be imprisoned many more times in South Africa and then in India for lengthy periods. Altogether, he spent over seven years in jail. After his release from his first imprisonment, he told a gathering of three thousand Indians in Johannesburg: "...I would rather pass the whole of my lifetime in gaol and be perfectly happy than to see my fellow-countrymen subjected to indignity..."[9]

 It was not a great step from this attitude of self-deprivation to the even more intense one of fasting. Although Gandhi's dietary regime included fasting, it was not until a strike by mill workers at Ahmedabad that Gandhi chose to fast as a symbolic gesture of solidarity. He had played a leading role in the strike, supporting the workers and urging nonviolence while also acting as their intermediary with the mill owners. But the workers' resolve was weakening and he decided that unless something drastic happened to rally them, their cause would be lost. He decided to fast until a settlement was reached. The dispute was quickly finalized the following day. Gandhi, however, was to fast on many other occasions: to protest the killing of civilians in Bombay after political riots left fifty-eight dead and hundreds injured; a number of times in support of the Untouchables; and most dangerously in the 1942-43 "Quit India" campaign to oust the British, when his twenty-one day fast brought him close to death. To the viceroy he wrote, "...if I do not survive the ordeal ... [p]osterity will judge between you as a representative of an all-powerful government and me a humble man who tried to serve his country and humanity through it."[10]

The mid- to late-1940s in India were a desperate time when hundreds of thousands died in riots and street battles as Hindus and Muslims fought in the lead-up to independence. The Muslims under Muhammad Ali Jinnah wanted to partition off the northern part of India to create a homeland that would be called Pakistan. When savage fighting left hundreds dead throughout the country, Gandhi responded by walking barefoot from village to village through the Muslim region of Bengal, trying to allay fears and bring calm.

Although the political temperature eased, Gandhi warned the new viceroy, Lord Mountbatten, that any attempts to divide India would plunge the country into civil war. Jinnah, on the other hand, threatened civil war if partition did not go ahead. Fearing any further delays in independence, and hoping that the violence would subside, Jawaharlal Nehru, as leader of the Indian National

Congress, agreed to Jinnah's demands. Gandhi spent Independence Day in prayer, questioning if all that he had worked for had been in vain and fearful of what was to come. To his horror the violence continued. Soon half a million were dead and fifteen million homeless as refugees surged across the borders.

Toward the end of 1947 and into 1948, Gandhi traveled from Calcutta to the Punjab, where conditions in Delhi were so bad he had to stop his pilgrimage. Appalled by the violence, he entered his last fast, in support of Muslims in Delhi who had been dispossessed of their homes. By the third day, the seventy-nine-year-old Gandhi was seriously ill, and three days later doctors feared imminent kidney failure. On the morning of the sixth day a pledge arrived from all political leaders assuring Gandhi that the houses confiscated from Muslims would be returned. In light of this Gandhi broke his fast.

A few days later a Hindu extremist group detonated a bomb at one of Gandhi's prayer meetings. He was well aware that his life was under threat. "If I fall victim to an assassin's bullet," he vowed, "there must be no anger from within me. God must be in my heart and on my lips."[11] Ten days later, on January 30, 1948, Gandhi was assassinated at his morning prayer meeting. The man who preached tolerance and nonviolence died instantly from three bullet wounds.

Mike Nicol
Cape Town, 2006

AN EYE FOR AN EYE MAKES THE WHOLE WORLD BLIND.

An ideal is one thing; living up to it is quite another...
We may be said to have an ideal only when we put forth
an effort to realize it.

Strength does not come from physical capacity.
It comes from an indomitable will.

There are many causes that I am prepared to die for, but no causes that I am prepared to kill for.

We who seek justice will

 have to do justice to others.

We are all bound by the ties of love...

Scientists tell us that without the presence of the
cohesive force amongst the atoms that comprise this
globe of ours, it would crumble to pieces and we
would cease to exist, and even as there is cohesive
force in blind matter, so must there be in all things
animate, and the name for that cohesive force among
animate beings is love.

We notice it between father and son, between brother
and sister, friend and friend... Where there is love
there is life.

Our ability to reach unity in diversity will be the beauty and the test of our civilization.

Religions are different roads converging to the same point. What does it matter that we take different roads so long as we reach the same goal?

{ Written during a return voyage from
London to South Africa

1908}

YOU MUST BE THE CHANGE YOU WISH TO SEE IN THE WORLD.

I wanted to avoid violence. Nonviolence is the first article of my faith. It is also the last article of my creed. But I had to make my choice. I had either to submit to a system which I considered had done an irreparable harm to my country, or incur the risk of the mad fury of my people bursting forth when they understood the truth from my lips. I know that my people have sometimes gone mad. I am deeply sorry for it and I am, therefore, here to submit not to a light penalty but to the highest penalty. I do not ask for mercy. I do not plead any extenuating act. I am here, therefore, to invite and cheerfully submit to the highest penalty that can be inflicted upon me for what in law is a deliberate crime, and what appears to me to be the highest duty of a citizen... I owe it perhaps to the Indian public and to the public in England... To the court too I should say why I plead guilty to the charge of promoting disaffection towards the Government established by law in India.

Affection cannot be manufactured or regulated by law. If one has no affection for a person or system, one should be free to give the fullest expression to his disaffection, so long as he does not contemplate, promote, or incite to violence. But the section under which mere promotion of disaffection is a crime. I have studied some of the cases tried under it; I know that some of the most loved of India's patriots have been convicted under it. I consider it a privilege, therefore, to be charged under that section.

In my opinion, noncooperation with evil is as much a duty as is cooperation with good. But in the past, noncooperation has been deliberately expressed in violence to the evildoer. I am endeavoring to show to my countrymen that violent noncooperation only multiplies evil, and that as evil can only be sustained by violence, withdrawal of support of evil requires complete abstention from violence.

{ Gandhi's statement in the Great Trial of 1922. He was charged with "bringing or attempting to excite disaffection towards his Majesty's Government established by law in British India" due to articles he wrote for *Young India*, one of the newspapers he founded. He was found guilty and sentenced to six years' imprisonment. }

1922

If we have no charity and no tolerance, we shall never settle our differences.

{Extract from *Young India*, April **1924**}

The desire to improve ourselves for the sake of doing good to others is truly moral. The highest moral law is that we should unremittingly work for the good of mankind.

To observe morality is to attain mastery over our mind and our passions.

A man is but the product of his thoughts; what he thinks, he becomes.

Real disarmament cannot come unless the nations of the world cease to exploit one another.

Genuine laughter is true eloquence

and more effective than speech.

FAIR MEANS ALONE CAN PRODUCE FAIR RESULTS.

.If we take care of the means, we are
bound to reach the end sooner or later.
When once we have grasped this point,
final victory is beyond question.
Whatever difficulties we encounter,
whatever apparent reverses we sustain,
we may not give up the quest for truth.

Terrorism and deception are weapons not of the strong but of the weak.

[There] is not a single offense which does not, directly or indirectly, affect many others besides the actual offender. Hence, whether an individual is good or bad is not merely his own concern but really the concern of the whole community, nay, of the whole world.

{ Extract from the Congress Party presidential address, December

1924 }

Truth is not to be found by anybody who has not got an abundant sense of humility.

There is no happiness like truth, no misery like untruth.

TRUTH NOURISHES THE SOUL. UNTRUTH CORRODES IT.

No matter how insignificant the thing
you have to do, do it as well as you
can, give it as much of your care and
attention as you would give to the thing
you regard as most important. For it
will be by those small things that you
shall be judged.

The more efficient a force is, the more silent and the more subtle it is. Love is the subtlest force in the world.

The law of love governs the world. Life persists in the face of death. The universe continues in spite of destruction going on. Truth triumphs over untruth. Love conquers hate.

To conceal ignorance

is to increase it.

Truth resides in every human heart, and one has to search for it there and to be guided by truth as one sees it. But no one has a right to coerce others to act according to his own view of truth.

THE POLICY OF RETALIATION HAS NEVER SUCCEEDED.

The straight path is as difficult as it is simple. Were it not so, all would follow the straight path.

Do not crave to know the views of others, nor base your intent thereon. To think independently for oneself is a sign of fearlessness.

Power based on love is a thousand times more effective and permanent than the one derived from fear of punishment.

One thing is certain. If the mad race for armaments continues, it is bound to result in a slaughter such as has never occurred in history. If there is a victor left, the very victory will be a living death for the nation that emerges victorious. There is no escape from the impending doom save through a bold and unconditional acceptance of the nonviolent method with all its glorious implications.

When a man gives way to anger, he harms himself.

For the last twenty years we have tried to learn not to lose courage even when we are in a hopeless minority and are laughed at. We have learned to hold on to our beliefs in the confidence that we are in the right. It behoves us to cultivate this courage of conviction, for it ennobles man and raises his moral stature.

{ Extract from the "Quit India" speeches, August

1942 }

GIVE ALL, GAIN ALL.

There are moments in your life when you must act even though you cannot carry your best friends with you. The still small voice within you must always be the final arbiter when there is a conflict of duty.

My work will be finished, if I succeed in carrying conviction to the human family that every man or woman, however weak in body, is the guardian of his or her self-respect and liberty.

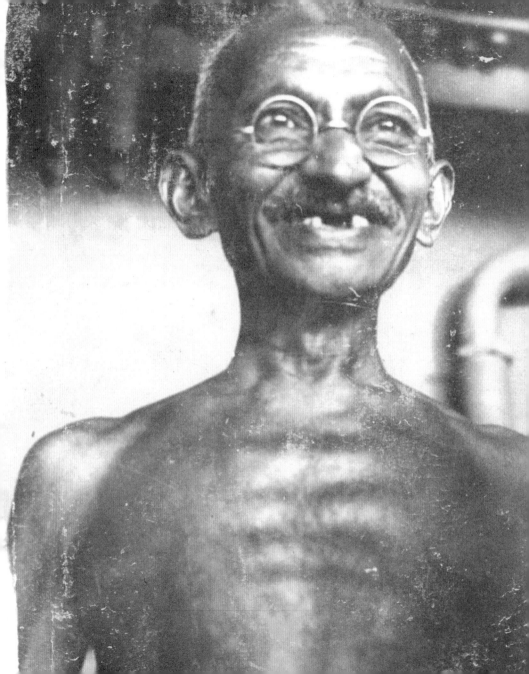

HE WHO LOSES HIS INDIVIDUALITY LOSES ALL.

No man loses his freedom except

through his own weakness.

I feel in the innermost recesses of my heart, after a political experience extending over an unbroken period of close upon thirty-five years, that the world is sick unto death of blood-spilling. The world is seeking a way out...

{ Extract from a radio address in London, September

1931}

Real education consists in drawing the best out of yourself.

It is a bad habit to say that another man's thoughts are bad and ours only are good and that those holding different views from ours are the enemies.

Justice needs to be tempered with generosity as much as generosity needs to be tempered with justice.

EVERY GOOD DEED IS ITS OWN ADVERTISEMENT.

Outward peace is useless

without inner peace.

If we are to make progress, we must not repeat history but make new history. We must add to the inheritance left by our ancestors.

CHARITY

A royalty from the sale of this book will be shared between the Tygerberg Children's Hospital and Philani Clinic on behalf of Archbishop Desmond Tutu, and the Navajivan Trust.

ACKNOWLEDGMENTS

The publisher is grateful for permissions to reproduce material subject to copyright. Every effort has been made to trace the copyright holders and the publisher apologizes for any unintentional omission. We would be pleased to hear from any not acknowledged here and undertake to make all reasonable efforts to include the appropriate acknowledgment in any subsequent editions.

Words of Mahatma Gandhi copyright © Navajivan Trust. Used with permission. Images used with permission of the following copyright holders: p. 2 © Matt Hoyle; pp. 6, 9, 10, 13, 14, 17 (also cover), 18, 21, 56–57, 71, 78 and 85 © Getty Images; p. 33 © Time Life Pictures/Getty Images; p. 50 © AFP/Getty Images.

The publisher would like to thank the following people and organizations.

Archbishop Tutu for his generous support of the Ubuntu Collection; and Lynn Franklin, Archbishop Tutu's literary agent, for her kind assistance with the series.

The Navajivan Trust, and in particular Jitendra Desai, Managing Trustee. The Trust, which was founded by Mahatma Gandhi in 1929, holds copyright on all his writings, the income from which is used to further Gandhi's work.

Mike Nicol for his insightful biographical essay. Mike Nicol has had a distinguished career both in South Africa and in the UK as an author, journalist, and poet. He is the author of four critically acclaimed novels published in South Africa, the U.S., the UK, France, and Germany. His best-known nonfiction work is his book on *Drum* magazine, *A Good-Looking Corpse* (Secker & Warburg, 1991), widely regarded as one of the most compelling accounts of the vibrant culture in the black townships of the 1950s.

Thanks also to Jenny Clements for text research and Simon Elder for picture research.

SELECT BIBLIOGRAPHY

Bush, Catherine, *Mohandas Gandhi* (Burke Publishing Company, London, 1988).
Chadha, Yogesh, *Rediscovering Gandhi* (Century Books, London, 1997).
Fischer, Louis (ed.), *The Essential Gandhi — An Anthology* (Random House, NY, 1962).
Gandhi, M. K., *Hind Swaraj — Indian Home Rule* (Navajivan Trust, Ahmedabad, India, 1938).
— *An Autobiography or The Story of My Experiments with Truth* (Beacon Press, Boston, 1957).
— *All Men are Brothers — Life and Thoughts of Mahatma Gandhi as told in his Own Words* (Navajivan Trust, Ahmedabad, India, 1960).
— *A Thought for the Day* (Ministry of Information and Broadcasting, New Delhi, India, 1968).
— *The Selected Works of Mahatma Gandhi; Vol. 6 The Voice of Truth*, (Navajivan Trust, Ahmedabad, India, 1968).
— *God is Truth* (Penguin, London, 2001).
— and Jack, Homer A. (ed.), *The Gandhi Reader — A Source Book of his Life and Writings* (Grove Press, New York, 1961).
Swan, Maureen, *Gandhi: The South African Experience* (Ravan Press, Johannesburg, 1985).

NOTES FOR THE BIBLIOGRAPHIC ESSAY

1 Chadha, Yogesh, *Rediscovering Gandhi*, 290; 2 Ibid. 291; 3 Ghandi, M. K., *God is Truth*, 445 ; 4 Ibid. 28; 5 Ibid. 23; 6 Ibid. 114; 7 Ibid. 133; 8 Chadha, Yogesh, *Rediscovering Gandhi*, 326; 9 Ibid. 133; 10 Ibid. 388; 11 Bush, Catherine, *Mohandas Gandhi*, 98.

Other quotations are from the following sources: pp. 25, 27 (bottom) and 28 — Gandhi, M. K., *An Autobiography or the Story of My Experiments with Truth*; pp. 27 (top), 44–45, 52 (bottom), 53, 60–61, 66, 72, 75, 79, 87 (bottom) and 90–91 — Gandhi, M. K., *A Thought for the Day*; pp. 30–31, 35, 42 (bottom) and 47 — Gandhi, M. K., *Hind Swaraj — Indian Home Rule*; pp. 32, 34, 41, 43 (top), 49, 59, 69, 76, 87 (top) and 89 — Fischer, Louis, *The Essential Gandhi — An Anthology*; p. 37 — www.mahatma.org.in; pp. 38–39, 51 and 74 — Gandhi, M. K., *The Selected Works of Mahatma Gandhi; Vol. 6 The Voice of Truth*; pp. 42 (top), 43 (bottom), 48, 53 (top), 55, 63, 65, 70, 77, 84 and 92 — *All Men are Brothers — Life and Thoughts of Mahatma Gandhi as told in his Own Words*; pp. 80–81 and 83 — Gandhi, M. K., *The Gandhi Reader — A Source Book of his Life and Writings*.